Just One More Hug

Just One More Hug

A *For Better or For Worse*® Collection

by Lynn Johnston

Andrews, McMeel & Parker
A Universal Press Syndicate Company
Kansas City • New York

*L*ynn was wondering who to ask to do the introduction to this, her latest book. She felt it should be somebody famous, but she couldn't think of anyone famous who reads her comic strip that she could ask. So I said, "How about me?" My wife is not very good at remembering names, so she said, "Who?" "Me, Rod Johnston. You've heard of me, haven't you?" She said yes to that. "So I must be pretty famous if even you know who I am."

I'd like to start off by saying that I have always been regarded as a bit of a character, but it wasn't until after I married Lynn that I realized I could be a mold for a cartoon character! Or that what we did with some of our leisure time could result in more little characters. But I have to say it's been an enjoyable treat. I ran into a dentist friend whom I hadn't seen since we graduated. As soon as we met, he said, "I know all about you!" It made me realize that readers think the characters in the strip correspond exactly to members of our family. It certainly made me pay more attention to editing Lynn's strips.

Lynn and I have found that we are not alone in the trials and tribulations of having a family. Nothing has happened to us that hasn't happened already to someone else in North America. We have never had a game plan for organizing our family, and when we meet couples who plan not to have kids, but rather to have a "lifestyle," we wonder if we have done the right thing—particularly on "one of those days." And of course we always say, "Well, they'll be sorry when they're old and gray and have no children." Of course those couples have yet to show any signs of remorse.

Meanwhile, we survive each day wondering if we are being fair to our kids. We get mad about dumb things that maybe we shouldn't—after all, mud washes off the carpet. We hope above hope that the kids will turn out okay. When I feel most insecure about parenting, I often open up one of the For Better or For Worse collections. For me, it's like a scrapbook, and I realize that we are doing all right, and what's more . . . we are having fun. If it weren't for kids, what would we have to talk about at parties?

Which reminds me . . . when it's time to put the kids to bed, they think of anything possible to stall, but Lynn and I are pretty sharp. We catch on to most of their ploys—the "have to brush my teeth, have to go to the bathroom, can't find my teddy" tactics. But the one that neither Lynn nor I can ever quite resist is that most fantastic of all bedtime stalls— "Just one more hug!"

—ROD JOHNSTON

20

23

27

29

33

34

37

41

44

Panel 1: AUNTE BEV—LIZZIE GOT CHASED BY THE ROOSTER AGAIN TODAY!

Panel 2: HMM.... HE'S BEEN PRETTY ORNERY SINCE THE HENS DISAPPEARED.

Panel 3: YEP, HE'S GOT NOTHIN' TO DO—SO HE JUST GOES AROUND MAKIN' A DARNED NUISANCE OF HIMSELF.

Panel 4: ..... SOUNDS LIKE GRAMPA VERN AFTER HE RETIRED.

Panel 5: HOW DID THE HENS DISAPPEAR, UNCLE DANNY?

OINK WOOF SNUFF

Panel 6: WELL ...... THEY KEPT FALLING ASLEEP ON THE SIDES OF THE PENS ...... AN' THE PIGS ATE 'EM.

Panel 7: JUST LIKE THAT? —WOW!!

Panel 8: —YEAH, MIKE ...IT'S A PIG-EAT-CHICKEN WORLD!

45

47

49

59

REALLY? – YES, HE DID GET LOOSE FOR A WHILE THE OTHER DAY....

THAT WAS THE VET – FARLEY'S GOING TO BE FINE! – HE JUST ATE SOMETHING THAT MADE HIM SICK.

THERE'S EVEN A NAME FOR IT – "GARBAGE GASTRITIS"...

–AND I WANT NO JOKES ABOUT MY COOKING!!

HE'S A LITTLE SLOW, JUST YET – BUT HE'S FEELING FINE!

HOW CAN WE MAKE SURE HE DOESN'T GET SICK LIKE THIS AGAIN?

WELL, YOU CAN EITHER KEEP HIM IN YOUR OWN BACK YARD, MRS. PATTERSON...

–OR ASK YOUR NEIGHBORS TO PUT OUT BETTER QUALITY GARBAGE.

NOBODY'S PLAYING WIF ME.

EVERYBODY'S PLAYING WIF FARLEY. THEY KEEP HUGGING HIM AN' TALKING TO HIM....

JUST 'CAUSE HE WAS SICK. THAT'S WHY EVERYBODY LIKES HIM BEST.

....DADDY? – I DON'T FEEL WELL.

63

73

79

SO-TELL ME, ELLY- WHAT'S HAPPENING BETWEEN TED AND CONNIE?

OH, ANNE-HERE WE ARE AGAIN-GOSSIPING ABOUT POOR CONNIE.

IT'S NOT GOSSIP, ELLY! WE CARE ABOUT HER! WE UNDERSTAND HER! WE'RE HER BEST FRIENDS!

NOW! GIMME THE DIRT!

ELLY-IF TED IS STILL BEING A JERK.... WHY DOESN'T CONNIE JUST KISS HIM GOODBYE?

SHE FIGURES HE'LL CHANGE, I GUESS. WITH ENOUGH TALKING AND UNDERSTANDING, THINGS WILL WORK OUT.

TROUBLE IS, SHE'S DOING ALL THE TALKING AND UNDERSTANDING.

MOM? YOU HAFTA GO OUT AGAIN?

I'M GOING TO ANOTHER LIBRARY MEETING, ELIZABETH. IT'S IMPORTANT.

MORE 'PORTANT THAN ME?

NOW AN' THEN .... I HIT HER WITH A GOOD ONE!

111

117